10 ridiculously simple tips

Resume Writing

Straightforward Information in Condensed Format

★ ARTISTIC / BUSINESS SERIES ★
created by John DeGaetano

ARTISTIC / BUSINESS SERIES
created by John DeGaetano

About the Series

The "*ridiculously simple*" series is designed to give you straightforward information on a variety of subjects in a condensed format. These books help you be yourself, and guides your vision on the artistic side of your personality as relates to a business setting. Most experts agree that art finds it's way into the hearts of many, however to make it as an artist and do whatever it is you truly love, the business side always comes into play… and vice versa. How you treat your business side of things is really the key to success.

About this Book

10 Ridiculously Simple Tips: Resume Writing touches on all the things you need to know about writing a great resume for yourself and ultimately get the job of your dreams or help someone else write a fantastic resume. We'll give you 10 of the most important tips to consider when determining exactly what to plan for in content along with style considerations as it relates to the various types of businesses.

Putting the Pieces Together

Don't worry, you're not alone… putting the pieces together and writing a really great resume is intimidating for everyone.

What makes the task of writing a resume so difficult is knowing what to include, what not to, what to highlight, what to de-emphasize, etc. If you truly want the position you're applying for, then writing it… is a necessity. Next comes the interview and how you handle yourself around senior management. Being your everyday self yet displaying focused enthusiasm is the best approach.

With a resume, there is such thing as going overboard with design. Formatting should be subtle enough so that your application does not end up a rejection pile.

What does Wikipedia say?

Résumé

résumé (/ˈrɛzʊmeɪ/, rez-u-may or /rɛzʊˈmeɪ/; less frequently /ˈrɛzjʊmeɪ/ or /rɛzjʊˈmeɪ/; French: [ʁezyme]),[a] also spelled resume, is a document used by a person to present their backgrounds and skills. Résumés can be used for a variety of reasons, but most often they are used to secure new employment. A typical résumé contains a "summary" of relevant job experience and education, as its French origin (and its translation into Spanish as "resumen") implies. The résumé is usually one of the first items, along with a cover letter and sometimes an application for employment, which a potential employer sees regarding the job seeker and is typically used to screen applicants, often followed by an interview.

The curriculum vitae (CV) used for academic purposes in the UK (and in other European countries) is more akin to the résumé—a shorter, summary version of one's education and experience—than to the longer and more detailed CV that is expected in U.S. academic circles. Generally, the résumé is substantially shorter than a CV in English Canada, the U.S. and Australia.

As has been indicated above, the word résumé comes from the French word résumé meaning "summarized" or "summary". Leonardo da Vinci is credited with the first résumé though his "résumé" takes the form of a letter written about 1481–1482 to a potential employer, Ludovico Sforza.

*Information above courtesy of Wikipedia, the free encyclopedia.

Interesting Facts

There you are… submitting your resume, sometimes thinking you wish you had a dollar for every time you've actually done so. The fact is HR professionals and hiring managers sometimes receive hundreds of resumes for any given position, and on average will spend about 10-30 seconds on yours. So organizing information incorrectly could cost you a shot at an interview. This is the most common mistake made by job seekers.

Prospective employers want to see just the facts, rather than fluffy loose terms that lack objective meaning. You should include as many specific numbers as possible in your resume to quantify your achievements. For example, don't say that you substantially increased revenue in your department. Say that you increased revenue by 65 percent. Instead of saying you were the top salesperson on your team, say you averaged more than a half-million dollars in sales each year.

In all of these cases the viewer can clearly see the value of the individual and can quantify your potential, which actually puts you into the elite few. This one simple format sets you a part from the hundreds of resumes being viewed for a single position.

You do not need to take the hard sell approach either or make any claims that are not absolutely true. You do need to toot your own horn through... People more often get hired based on their presentation on paper and in-person rather than who is best suited for the position... believe it or not.

<u>The Good News:</u> is... if you are willing to learn how to create an excellent resume, with a little extra effort, you will usually get an even better response from prospective employers than people with better credentials.

Statistics

So why is a resume so important? Based on their records, the U.S. Bureau of Labor and Statistics summarizes the employers chief goal is to attract, motivate and retain the most qualified employees and match them to jobs for which they are best suited, and can be translated into dollars and cents.

*"A resume reflects the potential work
an employer can expect from you."*

This can mean that a position is sometimes filled based on previous task load regardless of experience. You see, in an ideal world, you are a good candidate if you already possess the exact skills the business needs. But, in today's competitive labor market however, demand for skilled workers far exceeds supply. So your previous performance can also set you above the rest even if you're lacking the necessary skills for the position.

It's now estimated that 42% of skills-based learning actually goes on within the organization. Some employers would rather give you their version of the exact training you need therefore this statistic opens up and encourages applying in a variety of industries.

Tips...

OK then, after your objectives are determined, prioritize the content of your resume to suit those objectives. You have a small window of time to get the interest of a hiring manager so being brief and extremely focused is essential. A lengthy resume does not translate to higher qualifications; it may even encourage the reader to skim though or by pass the document just based on the sight of its length.

To successfully launch a truly great resume of your own, follow these 10 helpful tips:

Limit Your Resume to One Page

Yes, some will say it is perfectly fine to go into your experience in two or three pages if you have a lot to say… don't listen to them.

Stay with just one page. Furthermore not everything you've done needs to be listed here however everything needs to be true and somewhat relevant. What we mean by somewhat relevant is that your field of expertise may carry over to another industry or of similar work type. If you make it relevant, present it in your summary at the top of the page, then chances are good the recruiter will see the connection.

So then, what are recruiters looking for? Well, in one word "content" in the right order. But first let's backtrack, and that is to the vital part in understanding the resume review process and the recruiter or manager's situation; normally these individuals are under immense time pressures and working a tight deadline. Next, they are initially searching for just a few keywords in your resume.

Now with that said a poor presentation on paper could hide the most important part of your background and skills and stop your resume from being fully read. Also the impression may seem to be of poor standard in the mind of the viewer and can ultimately stop your application from going to the next stage.

Use a Layout that Works Best for You

A good presentation based on what works for your type of experience can attract the HR professional to the document the moment your resume is received and/or before other applicants. It communicates that you have skills needed for the position and beyond by just what is described in the text of your resume. It can also instantly give the recruiter a positive feel about you and ultimately get you that first interview.

Draft a layout that is best for you, but nothing fancy. Include **contact** information at the top, your key **objectives**, your **experience**, then **education**, and **skills** and **honors**… simple and in that order. Use 11 or 12 pt easy to read font like Helvetica, Times Roman or Ariel.

Viewers will heartlessly reject resumes that they are finding difficult to read or navigate through, as their time is precious. Jobseekers do not realize that the way their information is presented can often be of more value in getting to the next stage of the application process, than the information itself.

Break down your long detailed paragraphs with relevant facts and figures into short sections and lists. Make your resume as easy to read as possible. Professionals may toss your resume aside if it is filled with too much text. Sometime white space is a good thing.

In addition, you should prepare a basic resume that you can tailor to each individual position you may be applying for. This allows you to work in something that shows specific knowledge and demonstrates how your skills and experience align with that particular company.

Tailor Your Resume to the Type of Position

Usually, the person who makes the hiring decision is also the person who is responsible for the bottom line productivity of the project or department you hope to join. This person cares deeply how well the job will be done. You need to write your resume to appeal directly to them. So focus on the employers needs, not yours and tailor your resume exclusively to the type of position. Imagine yourself looking at the resume and you are doing the hiring… is there a fit?

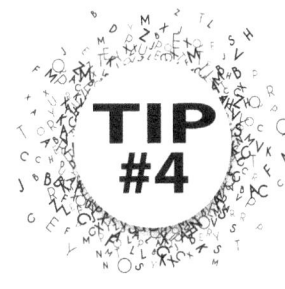

Maintain a Consistent Writing Style

Organization is the key word here. Your resume should be written with the most important information listed first. The body of your resume should start with your most recent professional experience, since it's generally the most relevant for the employer. The experience section should first include listing your most important accomplishments and strongest skills. This can create an immediate positive impression with the potential employer.

Believe it or not the time you have to persuade a prospective employer to read further and spend time on your resume is a little over 9 seconds, the equivalent of the attention span of goldfish. That's right, overall research estimates that only one interview is granted for every 200 or more resumes received by the average employer. This means that the reader may lose interest in your resume, upon which it is quickly scanned rather than read in its entirety.

This also means is that first impressions of your resume usually makes the decision to interview or not interview a candidate. As a result, the top half of the first page of your resume will either make you or break it for you. By the time the viewer has read the first few lines, you have either caught their interest, or your resume is set aside. So think of your resume as a piece of collateral or advertisement, there has to be motivation for the reader to act.

Make Sure the Information is Understandable

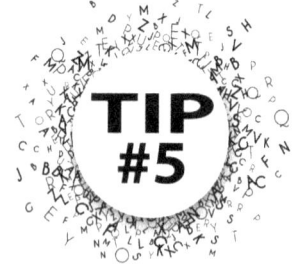

Use action words like the ones shown below. We've compiled this list to help your resume stand out. Avoid using the same verb over an over. If your resume is scanned electronically, the computer will understand and pick up on the words. Some companies now scan in your resume and have computers pull keywords that meet certain criteria. The computers are looking for one thing - the keywords that have been picked by the hiring manager. These are action keywords that relate to the position, so not including them or using shortened acronyms could mean your resume is disregarded as a "non-match".

102 ACTION WORDS

What are action words? Words like… "Achieved" or "consolidated" Use the following sample action words to enhance your resume and make your descriptions more powerful.

Achieved, activated, adapted, administered, advertised, advised, advocated, analyzed, appraised, assembled, attained, augmented, balanced, coached, collaborated, collected, communicated, compared, compiled, computed, consolidated, consulted, controlled, converted, coordinated, counseled, created, curtailed, decided, delegated, demonstrated, designated,

Designed, determined, developed, devised, directed, discovered, distributed, educated, eliminated, encouraged, endorsed, established, estimated, evaluated, examined, exchanged, executed, expanded, extended, formulated, governed, guided, illustrated, improved, increased, instructed, interpreted, introduced, invested, investigated, lectured, maintained, managed,

Measured, merged, minimized, modernized, modified, motivated, negotiated, observed, obtained, operated, organized, originated, oversaw, persuaded, planned, produced, promoted, publicized, published, recommended, replaced, reported, researched, restored, serviced, solved, sponsored, strengthened, studied, suggested, supervised, supplemented, surpassed, synthesized, taught, trained, updated.

Be Clear and Concise in Descriptions

To write an effective resume, you have to learn how to write powerful yet subtle content. Not only that, the item you're selling may be one you've invested an entire career in… that item is you. OK, selling your story is not exactly easy; you know… marketing side of yourself. But if you want to increase your job-hunting effectiveness as much as possible, it would be wise to learn how to write spectacular content.

You should always use descriptive %'s, $'s and #'s. The old saying is "safety in numbers and numbers don't lie" so with that in mind dollar totals, numbers, and percentages stand out in the body of a resume. Try writing a few lines that incorporates numbers… being specific does not mean it has to be long. Something like… "Manage increased cost savings of

8% in western region's 4 locations." Also, while you're at it, take the time to include a brief description of an organization that may not be recognizable.

Make Sure there are No Spelling Errors

You should proofread your resume at least two or three times. Don't depend on your spell-check, as it can miss words that may be spelled correctly but used in the wrong context. Have at least one other person proofread your resume. A fresh set of eyes can catch errors you might have missed. See tip #10 for more information in reviewing your resume before it is sent out.

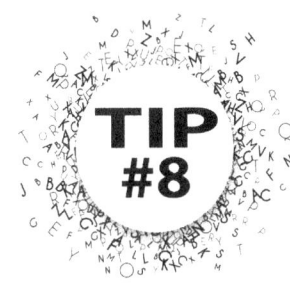

Be Consistent with The Entire Look

Some white space is important. Open up the newspaper, and take note of which ads first catch your attention. Are they the ads that are jammed full of text or are they ads that have a large amount of unused space (the term is- white space). This is done to grab your attention, as readers are always attracted to open areas. So don't worry if you are having a hard time filling the page with text; consider increasing or adjusting spacing of letters or characters within the page layout.

Use bullets with short sentences to structure the body of your resume. The main selling points of your resume should be clear and quick to scan. Again, don't worry about the specifics; you will go into much more detail during the interview. You should include a brief objective statement in the body of your resume.

Remember to highlight your strengths, and what is most relevant to the potential employer. Remember the time limit each resume is viewed even in the best of job markets so put forth the effort to determine which bullets points most strongly support your job search objective. Put the strongest and most relevant items first where they are more apt to be read. This is your hook, the stuff that lures the reader... and the rest of your resume reels them in.

Choose a Font that is Easy to Read

You may be tempted in an effort to have your resume stand out but don't use intricate fonts that are hard to read. Keeping your fonts standard will help combat conversion issues from PC to MAC or from one program version to another and is just simply easier to read.

Also remember to keep it concise, that it's not necessary to submit a resume that is more than one page. If you're not sure which resume format to use try a chronological resume format, use quality paper and clean copies. Also add a reference page and cover letter as an introduction displaying an example of your professionalism.

Think Outside the Box

You're on the road to a promising career! But before you start applying, get a second opinion. Ask a friend, for an outside opinion on your resume before sending it off. Have a friend subjectively review your resume since you are so close to your situation, it can be difficult for you to align all your high points and clearly convey all your accomplishments. Don't just settle for good… go for great content.

In today's changing economy, what was once a flourishing job market has now dried up into a very challenging and competitive wasteland. Always take comments and feedback into consideration, and revise your resume accordingly to improve your chances.

Above all… be positive in your resume and interview - you must be positive. Leave out negatives and irrelevant points. If you feel your graduation date or any dates will subject you to age discrimination, leave it out of your resume. If you do some duties in your current job that don't support your job search objective, don't include them. Focus on the responsibilities that do support your objective, and leave off irrelevant personal information. If nothing else, interviewing more and more will increase your interviewing skills.

OK, you're ready! Apply for jobs that appear to be above your qualifications, apply to positions that are a match and apply to positions that may be below your level. Why... because it may lead to a bigger and better opportunity. Like anything else, repetition will decrease your nervousness, and increase your skills at tackling tough questions. Remember: the interview is the place to elaborate on accomplishments, performance and build on your work-style. Not the resume.

One more note on content – make sure your resume contains everything the employer needs to be convinced that you are a good match for the position. To recap, a complete resume includes the following sections:

- Name and address
- E-mail address / Phone
- Objective Statement
- Employment History
- Education Information
- Other Information and Skills

Various Sources: Economic Trends and Research Data, Conference Board of Canada, United States, Learning & Development Outlook Report, International Workplace Education, Wikipedia, the free encyclopedia, Training Studies and Field Experience.

So There You Have It!
Guiding you on the best road to a great resume!

10 Ridiculously Simple Tips: Resume Writing

Resume Tips in Review
1. Limit Your Resume to One Page
2. Use a Layout that Works Best for You
3. Tailor Your Resume to the Type of Position
4. Maintain a Consistent Writing Style
5. Make Sure the Information is Understandable
6. Be Clear and Concise in Descriptions
7. Make Sure there are No Spelling Errors
8. Be Consistent with The Entire Look
9. Choose a Font that is Easy to Read
10. Think Outside the Box

About the Author

John DeGaetano – *on the business side, John is a certified business advisor and works with businesses in guiding them in creating economic impact in the form of sales, jobs and market analysis. On the artistic side, John is the artistic director of a theatre company non-profit organization and author of several full length and 10-minute plays. His stage director credits include; Cats, Pirates of Penzance, Joseph and the Amazing Technicolor Dreamcoat, Chicago, West Side Story, and Evita to name a few. He's assisted with numerous other productions such as Miss Saigon along with Radio and Television work. His plays, informational books and presentations are available on Amazon, bookstores, and elsewhere.*

John DeGaetano Productions

More titles in the
10 Ridiculously Simple Tips Series

Includes:

Audition for the Stage
Business Plans (coming soon)
Financial Projections (coming soon)
Marketing
Motivation
Resume Writing
Sales
Social Networking
Stage Production
Training

www.ingramcontent.com/pod-product-compliance
Lightning Source LLC
Chambersburg PA
CBHW071835200526
45169CB00018B/1533